The things

We

See

Along the way.

Along the Way

A Contemporary Poetry Anthology

Compiled by Guy Farmer

Cover Art by Carol Gilman

Opportunity Publishing

Copyright © 2018 Opportunity Publishing
All rights reserved.
ISBN: 1986742075
ISBN-13: 978-1986742078

To Carol

CONTENTS

Introduction

Poems

Wanda Morrow Clevenger

    Monkey Rum Punch   1

    Antipathy   2

    Yellow and Blue   3

    Whatever Analogy Works   4

    All-Inclusive   5

Gareth Culshaw

    The Smoker   7

    Mrs. Edwards   8

    A Pair of Difference   10

    Axe   11

    The Labourer   11

Steve Denehan

Galaxies	13
Daughter	14
Two Balconies in Santa Luzia	15
Lahinch, Fifteen Years Ago	17
The Sunniest Day	18

Naduni Dineisha

Daisies	20
An Educated Wife	21
To 'You' with Nostalgia	23
The Flower Auction	25
A Kandyan Wedding	27

Diane Woodward Dorff

Ever After	30
Peace and How to Travel There	32
A Note to Mr. Carnegie	34
Recapturing Fireflies	36
Tree Shadows	38

Robin Wyatt Dunn

What Avenue to Sleep I Made 40
Which Reach or Reason 41
Who Made the World 42
We're Gonna Play 42
Who Heard Me 43

J. K. Durick

Thought Train 45
Afternoons 46
Road-Kill 48
Adam 50
The Edge 51

Guy Farmer

Quiet Spaces 53
Reliving 54
As If Nothing 55
Shallow Blather 56
A Fine Evening 57

Ian Fletcher

At a Graduation Ceremony	58
Man of the Suburbs	59
Breakdown	60
Poet	61
Death in the Suburbs	62

Allison Grayhurst

Body of the Whale	64
Cardinal	67
Hooked	69
Fuller Octave Frequency	71
Rodents and Wings	74

Tara Lynn Hawk

Logs Needed	77
Check Out	77
Green Love Poem	78
Cur Non	79
The Science of Fire	79

Richard Kalfus

    Finding Our Humanity   81

    The Power of Touch   82

    Lament of the Aging   84

    An American Son   86

    She Survived   87

G. S. Katz

    Coffee and Cake, Vietnam, 1966   89

    Booths in Dark Restaurants   90

    Loner   92

    Being Right — a Poem about My Mom   93

    Fruit Man on the Corner   95

Sofia Kioroglou

    Treading Water   96

    Damascus in Syria before the War   96

    Through the Myrtle Fields   97

    Ode to Cyprus   98

    What I Call Poetry   99

Tricia Knoll

Body Language	100
The Night I Didn't Stand Up	102
Portland's Waterfront History	104
Let's Hear It for the Horses	106
Connecting	107

Joan Leotta

Not Your Everyday Venus	109
Resilience	110
Pax Americana Finis	111
Deciding Factor	112
Clouds	113

Marie MacSweeney

The Water Bowl	115
Gold Boat	117
The Flint Napper	119
Carrier Bag	121
Gold Hoard	123

Carolyn Martin

Along the Desert View Trail on Mount San Jacinto	126
Tourists at Re-Mudding Time	128
A Requiem in November	130
One Does as One Must	131
Elusive	133

Diane G. Martin

Summer Gardens	135
Nursery Rhyme	136
Over the Yardarm	139
Winterreise	140
Remembrance for Rosemary	142

Stan Morrison

What If	144
Drumbeat	145
Swamp People	146
Death at an Early Age	146
Politics and the English Language	148

Bonnie Burka Shannon

    The Numbers Game   149

    He Never Expresses Regret   150

    A Need to Travel   153

    The Actress   155

    Endings   156

Langley Shazor

    Shards of Glass   159

    Predilections   161

    Hand Crafted   162

    Paper Cuts   163

    Cosmos   164

Sravani Singampalli

    Life Is a Glass of Coke   166

    100 Opinions and Choices   166

    Summer 2011   169

    Unaware   170

    Mind and Body   171

Chloe Thompson

Willow Widow — 173
Dark Horse — 174
Patchwork Guilt — 176
No Story — 179
Captivating — 182

Niamh Twomey

Someday — 183
Face — 185
Curls — 186
First Memory — 187
She Remembers — 188

Poet Biographies — 193

About Opportunity Publishing — 215

INTRODUCTION

As I compiled this anthology, I was moved time and again by the feelings and insights the poems evoked in me. I'm pleased to say there's something in this collection for anyone who contemplates the human condition — from prehistory to modern day, intimate to vast. I'd like to thank the wonderful poets whose extraordinary creativity made this book possible and to you, the reader, who appreciates their art.

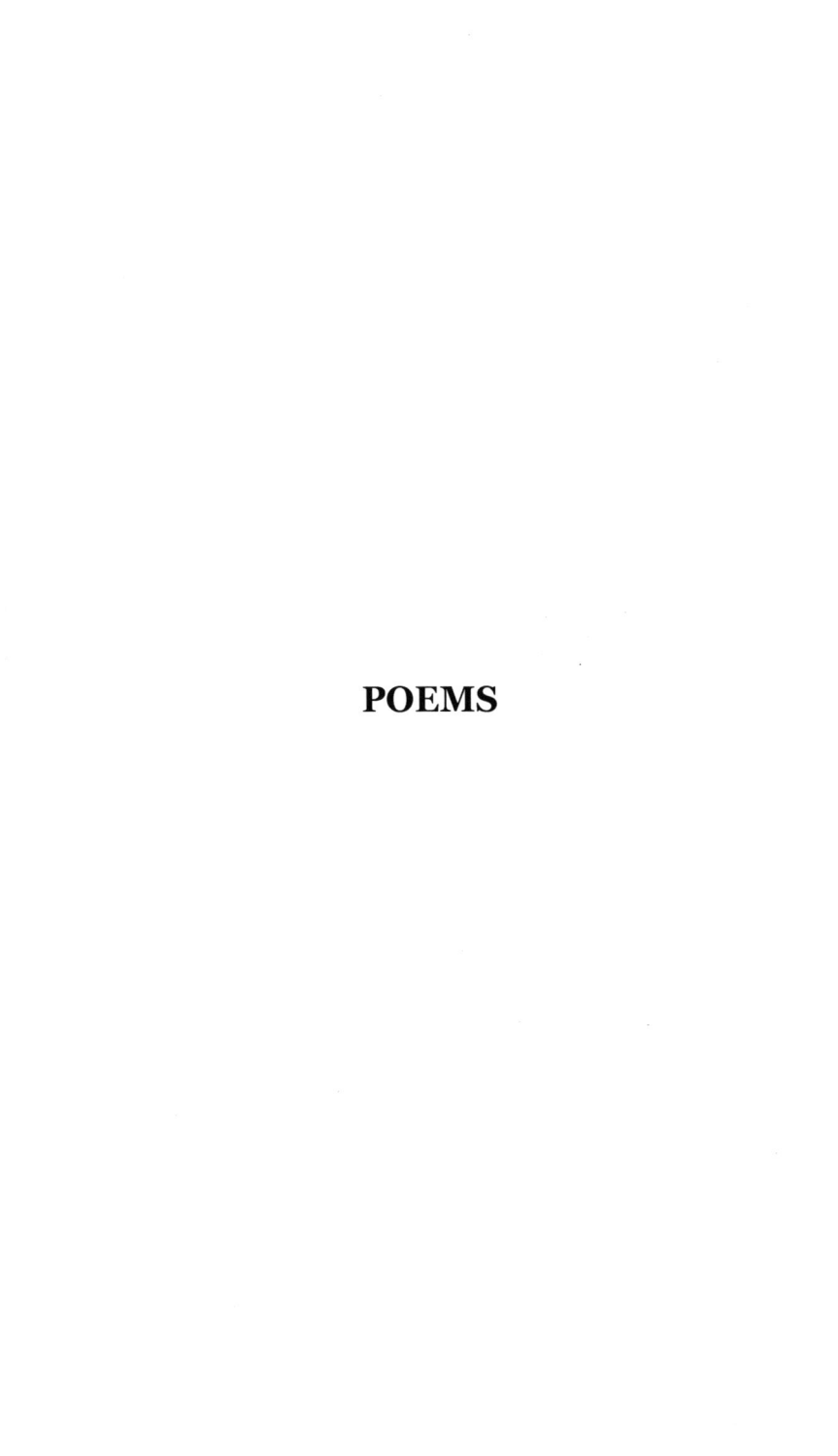

POEMS

Wanda Morrow Clevenger

Monkey Rum Punch

darkest blue
turns clear green
when you reach
mile marker zero

our tour guide
tells how Papa's
drinking buddies
helped him build
a retaining wall
with stolen bricks

up close the wall
remains monkey rum
punch wonky

Antipathy

her screed
spat onto the rewind
of my landline
where I left it
damning me to
vigorous wrath
>god was going
to get me<
would have been
laughable
had it not been

a red digital 1
reminded day
and night
on my birthday
on three consecutive
holidays how
god was going
to get me good

after six months
her hellfire
having failed
I deleted
the antipathy
the phone ever so
politely chimed
>you have no messages<

Yellow and Blue

balloons were released
at the small grave site

I like to think
they rise still

Whatever Analogy Works

hypoglycemia changes
its spots, its stripes
whatever analogy works

a full-court press sweat
or two or more
amoebalike white spots
merged into one
big white
blinding hole

a something's off
sinking swirling
lip tingling
anxiousness
or it's nothing first
black next, a distinctive
Isaac Newton thud

then it is waiting for

someone to find
your sweaty carcass
and stick the hypo
from the red case
into your arm

All-Inclusive

on the 4th day
we went ashore
at Freeport

a makeshift row
of souvenir shanties
a covered grub pub deck
and a private beach

our pink wrist bands
denoted we had paid
only for chairs
big umbrellas

and the view
of course

a boy given an all-
inclusive wrist band
fell down, rolled
got up, fell down
stayed down

his sister French-kissed
the sand twice

these siblings seated
by us on the bus back
were warily eyed, the
girl already out cold

the woman in front
of us turned to say
he's going to yak
for sure

Gareth Culshaw

The Smoker

She helped the elderly, smoked
in the car, in the kitchen, in the living
room, probably in the bath.

Her husband worked away. His knuckles
raw like used wrecking balls. His voice
filled her home when he was back.

She kept her head down and grinned
with a smile when she saw you. But it
was fake like a sky full of rainless clouds.

He walked around the garden like a guard
dog, lay on a sunbed and brought
the sun rays to his skin. She laughed

with a neighbour as they leaned on gates.

Her car was always in the corner of the street
to keep their house from moving away

in the night. He put up a fence around
the garden. Trimmed the hedge with worn
teeth. She lit up in the kitchen, boiled

the kettle, and poured him a cuppa
when he came in shirtless. His voice
filled her head, and she blew out his words

after every drag.

Mrs. Edwards

She never liked me,
I saw it in her eyes.
They were colourless
and when I looked at her
it felt like I was looking
down the barrel of a gun.

Her black hair was formal,
her voice a hammer
and anvil. I would sit in her
lessons with hands on my thighs.
Back straight, tongue resting.
My hand tried to pick up

the weight of the pen
ink its way into her heart.
She looked at me like a hawk
above a field, and my mouth
went dry, hands clammed up.
The classroom ceiling

balanced on my head,
stopped me from growing,
and finding myself within the walls.

A Pair of Difference

She looked the same as the wind touched.
I focused onto the frozen waterfalls
saw the weep of water wane.
There was a slowing down of erosion.

She looked the same as the wind touched.
And we walked across the stones.
The path ahead parted and we had to walk
one way or ignore the other.

She looked the same as the wind touched.
We shared the path, but were going different
routes. I watched my way then let her
go through the gate, before I closed it tight.

Axe

I watched him heave
the axe in a half moon
arc. He brought it down
with the force of wanting

to split the world in two.
So he could see if his father
was there, waiting in the next

The Labourer

He was a fermented apple
drinker. Lips used only for
holding a ciggie.

His throat a drainpipe
to flood his innards with
volume. Builder's helmet

sat on his head, lemon-coloured
just like his baccy-rolled fingers.
Steel toe capped boots

made heavier when he sat in them.
The beer glass by his bed
empty like the weekends

he has drunk through. A ceramic
grid sits in his mouth, allowing
the sun to shine into a pit of darkness.

Steve Denehan

Galaxies

I jump as high and as far as I can.
I hang in the air, beneath the sun, while the water,
waits,
to catch me.
I am nine years old, coiled springs inside me,
Fires sparked by lightning in my mind.

My body blanches for half a moment as the water takes me.
I look around in muffled silence.
Flotsam in the hazy blue, an underwater galaxy,
In which I am the sun.

Surfacing, I clamber out.
I am forty-two years old.

I am rusty springs and embers,
a grateful planet in a much younger life.

She splashes and giggles behind me.
She is the sun.

Daughter

You leaned in close and asked me to close my eyes.
I did so and began to smile, sure of something playful to come.
You asked me solemnly not to move my mouth. I tried.
Slowly, delicately, you traced a pattern under my left eye,
As if running the tiny pad of your finger along a spider web.
You told me to open my eyes.
They were met by your face, sorrowful and embarrassed.

You told me that you were touching my old age.
You smiled a little,
And forgave me.

Two Balconies in Santa Luzia

Our balconies were adjacent to each other
Each night, when time was our own, we would sit on ours,
Reading, greedy for the heat, unfamiliar on our Irish skin
They would eat late and the aromas would creep around to us
and tantalise
He sounded French, she, Portuguese, though they talked little
We heard their glasses clink on their glass-topped table.

The longest conversation we heard was their last.
First, the sound of a chair sliding on the terracotta tiles
Then, in accented English,
"I love you."
"I love you too."
"Tell them I fell."
As gravity pulled him down, he lived another second, maybe two
Then, he didn't.
He was a person
then
suddenly, he was a body.
She tried to scream but only a kind of strangled wheeze escaped her.
Our balconies were separated by a wall.
I could not see her.
There were a thousand miles between us.
"Are you okay?" I asked.

Lahinch, Fifteen Years Ago

I was wanted by the sea.
Desperately wanted.
I was taken out.
I was floating,
my feet far above solid ground.
Every part of me was ached for,
caressed, examined, desired.
The sea wanted to take me away
to inky darkness and salty cold,
and I,
was going.

Then, a voice,
louder than the sea's song.
Surfacing, I saw his face,
Felt his forearm around my shoulder.
A thief, stealing me from the sea.
So, they fought, both for me,
he and the sea.
To help, I kicked

and clawed at the waves
and then
he gasped
"Stop it...
...you...
...are...
...holding...
...me...
...back."

The Sunniest Day

Most of that day is lost to me.
I let it slip through my splayed fingers
Not happily, but eagerly.
Fragments remain, luminous detail,
Branded onto the lining of my mind.
The sun, daring me not to squint,
so bright as I walked toward it.
The flaking paint on our front door,
the creak as it opened and,

my "hello" trying to find you.

It was your shoes I noticed first, pristine,
saved for special occasions.
For nearly one whole heartbeat
I tried to ignore the fact that they
were two feet from the floor.

The conspicuous flatness of your belly
almost at my eyeline.
Then, that violent eruption of silence
pushing me to our chocolate-coloured carpet.

The paint still flakes on our front door.
I will paint it soon.
I promise.

It doesn't hurt because you left me,
it hurts
because I stayed.

Naduni Dineisha

Daisies

My mother grows daisies
In a patch near the garden wall
They are in full bloom
Under the scorching sun

Two rounds of tiny petals
Running around each golden centre
The daisies look lovely
Swaying in the warm breeze

After a few days
When I went to the patch
Some of the flowers were
Half-eaten by ants
Their beauty maimed,
Their freshness gone
They looked old and haggard

Ants have become predators and
The daisies prey
The innocent daisies
Who, before, swayed in the wind
Proudly in full bloom
Now bent with sorrow
Tried to make, in vain
The garden beautiful

An Educated Wife

You say I'm enigmatic and weird,
And ask whether I had ever met anybody 'matching'
When our married life is tensed.

I say no but I'm at a loss,
How can I be like somebody else?

How can I think conventionally,
When my consciousness knows better?

How can you expect me to be
Accepting + compliant = the ideal wife
And ask me to endure silently
Your unjustifiable dominance?
When it's you, when I was your student,
Who taught me otherwise?

I'm at a loss...
Tell me,
Why shouldn't I apply your theories
To my private life?

The chiding
'You are too hard and frigid!'
You chide me, your face ablaze with anger
'You are hypersensitive and sentimental!'
I argue back, reversing the chiding.
But my inner self knows,
I was too harsh on you
And I also know
That I have become hard and frigid
Like a plant that after intermittent beatings

Of the weather, grows into a massive tree that
Nothing can bend.
But all the same your sweetness,
Silliness and cuteness
Remind me how once I was.
You are several years older than me
Do I envy you for your inborn gentleness
Still living inside you,
Impervious to the forces of society?
No.
But I fear
It transforming you
Into me,
On a day not far away.

To 'You' with Nostalgia

When I heard that some of the boys were
arrested
For using drugs
I expected to see you today

So that I could make sure you were okay
And I did see you
I still can't believe that it was you
Yes, it was you — the new you
The 'you' made by those who were around you
High and wavering like a kite
Undecidedly, to either side
You came dragging your feet uphill
Your once luxurious hair, now,
Dried up like coconut fronds and
Your once taut muscles, now,
Atrophied and saggy
You looked like a fish
With sunken cheeks and protruding cheek bones
You smiled at me
A disrespectful smile
Wagging your tongue and flirtatiously blinking
If a sane friend of mine did that I would have stopped him and asked

'Is this the way you greet a friend?'
But I just smiled with you
A polite, friendly smile
Not sneering, sympathising or demeaning
Just a kind smile that
I would give to any friend
I turned back and watched you go up the hill
Floating like a kite
I remembered the cautious, shy smiles
I used to receive those days

The Flower Auction

On the Il full moon Poya day
A day dedicated to Lord Buddha and his teaching
A grand auction is
Taking place in the village temple
An auction of flowers
The highest bid
Claims a basket full of jasmines

They are not very fresh
They have been on the auctioneer's table
For hours waiting for the highest bid
Or is it the heat from the bodies of sinful men
That have made them limp?

One thousand, three thousand, six thousand rupees
The plastic basket of home-grown jasmines
Shines with pride
From within the shrine room
The statue of Lord Buddha
Whose eyes never close
Patiently observes,
The richest vendor in the village,
Paying the sum,
Confiscates the jasmines

A Kandyan Wedding

I went to the wedding of two lecturers from
the low-country
Theirs was an up-country-style wedding and
I later discovered why

He was dressed in a royal blue 'sulu
aenduma'
The formal attire of ancient Sinhala kings
and ministers
His bride was dressed in a white Kandyan
To reflect her purity
He once said that he would marry
Only an upper-caste virgin
The white was his way of showing that

She reminded me of his first girlfriend
Who once came to meet him
Wearing a cheap white blouse
That emphasised the paleness of her drawn,
Elongated face and body

I overheard her begging him to
Accept her and his child

She too had once dreamed
Of wearing a white Kandyan and holding his hand
The proud way his young bride did that day
When he went to that poor girl's little house in Trincomalee
When he was struggling to find a job
It was she who comforted him and earned for both of them
By working in a factory that manufactured garments

She too was once pure,
Pure until he violated it
She is now his son's mother
His son now seven years old.
She is unmarried and who would marry her now?
She is unemployed

(She has no degree like his young lecturer-
bride)
Who would employ her?
He wanted a bride that equals him now in
every way
To climb, further, the social ladder

Diane Woodward Dorff

Ever After

Once upon a time when I was young,
I believed in fairy tales.
I knew my life would open like a scroll;
And every day enchantment waited
Somewhere in the silver air.
I thought I knew the part that I would play.
I listened for the song to cue my entrance,
And I believed in magic.
My prologue promised balladry,
The verses tumbling out.
My players slept in the enchanted forests
Until their time to wake.
And I knew which ones were mine
By the dialogue they spoke.
And so I lived the tale. Or tried.

But life I think is not a fairy tale,

but so much more;
with pages infinite as dreams.
Life, I think, is unforeseeable, unknown;
Full of unexpected verses;
Streaming through the maze of mornings.
Life is not a glittering tale of fairies.
It is a serial, its verses continually renewing,
Flying beyond, behind each other,
And filled with endless iterations.
No one knows the ending, and no one has the cues.
Characters arrive and dance among their stories,
Beyond descriptions on the page,
In endless possibility.

So I will leave my umbrella in its place at home.
I do not need a thing between the sky and me.
Release the parking brake,
for life is not emergency.

Let me be delivered from the fairy tale, the
fable, myth.
And let my life unwind itself in astonishment,
Blessed stumbling along the way.

Peace and How to Travel There

to all who travel with me

my soul is twisting
judging me and begging you
to release me from pain
to say I am absolved
I am understood
I am esteemed still

but I know that is not what I need
I need me to say
I am absolved
that I do not need absolving
I am simply me

trying to do the best I can
as are you

and I know
I am real and whole and good
no matter what you think
or I think you think

we are all struggling to be right
to be certified free from defect

but we are not
we are human

and we are trying
and I am trying
and I am me
and that is enough

A Note to Mr. Carnegie

At the 1916 dedication of the Belleville
Illinois Public Library, attendees were given
note cards and asked to write thank you
notes to Andrew Carnegie.

I've traveled
like your trains,
speeding out from your bricklaid library
carelessly following the tracks.
Hurtling myself
to a destination barely guessed;
rail after rail flying out behind me.

Before the beautiful libraries,
you were host to powerful locomotives
burning wood, then coal,
and spewing cinders.

And then the libraries.
You laid buildings like tracks

around the nation.
Depots for curious minds.
Safe passage for the dreamers

Thank you for the answers,
but more by far the questions,
your library gifted me.
Thank you for the kin I found,
companions of the stacks;
Americans who built the books,
who laid the tracks
and stoked the engines.
Transportation to anywhere
without a ticket.

Sandburg, Frost, and Emerson
Dickinson and Whitman;
the station masters,
American conductors, travelers themselves.

And up above the libraries,
the stars shone as they shine now,

on the heads of the readers;
of the travelers of the mind;
who know no walls and no restrictions.
Though iron rails may rust,
the routes whose crossroad is the library
go on forever.

Recapturing Fireflies

June evenings in
the yard of my girlhood;
Thick clouds of summer mist
skimmed the grass,
breathing green and heavy
on the threshold of summer.

I observed the rite of fireflies.

When I ran
In the darkening sea of air,
I drew the summer

into my lungs, and ran
through the grass sparkling with stars.

Chasing fireflies.

A dot of light in the velvet darkness,
inexplicable,
stitching the darkness together
with bits of sparkling thread.

And the tiny flash is woven
Into my soul,
a burst of yellow,

incendiary.

In the flicker of light,
the knowledge of children,
listening to fiery conversations.

Fireflies on the lawn;
a secret that

whispers me home again.
Ancient beacon
of my girlhood.
My daughter runs,
immersed in the dark,
hungrily looking for fireflies.
And because the fireflies' light
still lives behind my eyes,
we run together.

Tree Shadows

shadows on the grass.
patterns cast by the shadows of trees;
unfixed, unstable, impermanent, and brief.
shifting with sun and clouds and breath of wind.
patterns placed on summer lawns;
diagrams of beautifully disordered order.
webs spun from sunlight and chlorophyll;
in shades of green

tracery of leaves moving in the wind;
trunks and limbs and stems.
filigree of light and shadow.
lovely and mottled and shuddering,
and sad and beautiful in turns;

like all our memories,
like all our days.

Robin Wyatt Dunn

What Avenue to Sleep I Made

what avenue to sleep I made
the roar and arc of my weight
over the apartment
over the department of the soul
which reaches my keyboard
and you

I didn't know what beacon creeped under my
bed
tickling my feet
the made milk and rain
of the shore of our ruin
more glorious with each passing day

Which Reach or Reason

which reach or reason
mazing the mind for its dreams of love
inescapable
rank and ruffled musty splashed colored
under the grave levitating dead
my own nightmare and running start

each portion of the love would be
manhandled
bent
caught and trembling
for whose
and what's
divinity

not anything out of the ordinary
or normal

caught on the wall
unable to stop speaking

Who Made the World

who made the world
throw down over your feet
the awning of the stage

painted dry and radiant over their faces
not any picture
nor memory

the rift of the dust
the roar of the dove

storming your desire

We're Gonna Play

We're gonna play
badminton and ice hockey
chess and tag and hide and seek
handball and baseball

gonna see the new ThunderCats movie
and paint our faces

over the river is the moon
like an old god laughing

you can laugh with it too

Who Heard Me

who heard me
was it you?
the paint flowed over your face
iridescent
calked with brine
arbor and rift underneath the glee
carbon birth for watch and fate
cart bake and turn the youth underneath the
barrier
underneath the naked will
bent and unattached

luminous

rising over the fog
lightning and sun

the marriage of the dawn with the remnants
of your dreams:

exotic knife with arms
and legs

fleeing the city of your birth
and your name

into delight

"Who Heard Me" appeared in *1947 Journal* on February 18, 2017.

J. K. Durick

Thought Train

It's still there late at night, disturbing, insistent
upgrades and down, chugging, rattling, reminder

drawing some cargo, but empty most often now
worrying the tracks, the blind crossings, the faults

its ties and roadbed giving way under the years
the neglect, the expenses, the mounting debt

the dark can't swallow it all, the working engine
the cattle cars and coal cars, the sealed freights

the ghost cars, the long shadows it pulls with it
its chorus of loose bolts and boards keeping time

the screaming, whispering wail passing along

the deserted stations, the missing passengers

almost invisible until it awakens us this late
tickets in hand we line up, wait restlessly

jostle our luggage, all elbows and schemes
ready to board once again, ready to ride on,
night becomes our darkness to hold, to haunt,
the conductor smiles and begins our tickets,

there's more journey than destination in all this.

Afternoons

There's nothing memorable about them
Lining up the way they do — day after day,
like the ticks of a wind-up clock, or the ticks
On an old dog's belly, the ones we'd tweeze
Off and squeeze the life from and feel as if
Our time had been well spent. We could sleep
Walk our way through most of them, beating

The hum-drum drum of 'em, like thumbing
Our way across the Midwest, acres and acres
Flattened out as far as we're willing to see,
As flat as our spare tire, or, for that matter, our
Life line. They can be numbing and strumming,
Like the tunes old appliances play all day, or
Those songs that get trapped in our heads, like
Stormy weather, whether or not we're together
Or alone waiting, waiting for the telephone to
Ring, and then we begin to sing the one line we
Recall of that childhood song about the livelong
Day, as if we could get children prepared for
This, this afternoon of our discontent, this
Last nail in the coffin of usefulness. It's like
Waiting in a crowded waiting room and never
Being next, or standing in a line that never
Moves up an inch, or mowing an endless lawn
With a faulty mower that skips and skips but
Will never turn off. Afternoons are like those
Meetings about the by-laws, like a lecture on
Life insurance or retirement benefits. They're
The excuse we use between the mornings and

The evenings, the uphill climb of our work time,
The part of the day we while away, the only
Time we spend wishing it would end.

Road-Kill

Just beyond Bethel on 89, going 70 or so, I ran over a fox.
I couldn't swerve, couldn't slow. It happened way too fast.

Now, it sounds simple and small in the greater theater of
Things that happen like that: too slow, too fast to stop,

Laws of nature, laws of physics coming into play, survival
Of the quickest, moving objects of unequal size colliding.

But for that moment, the moment just before we hit, I saw
It all coming, I saw the amazing beauty of the animal, his or

Her energy, the beauty of its strength and movement. I saw
What seemed to be its desperation just as it disappeared and
Became another one of those lumps by the side of the road,
Lifeless, shredded, a thing we drive around, sometimes joke

About, leave to crows and flies, to highway crews charged with
Cleaning up our inconvenient, disturbing messes, the lessons
We leave behind. I heard a small thump under the tires, front
And back. It wasn't a skunk, so anything it left, like blood, or

Fur, or guts must have worn off the tread
almost immediately,
But the image of that fox and its last moment
stay with me.

Adam

How could he tire of this, lying out
on warm nights on a perfectly trimmed lawn;
for company, perhaps a dog or two
listening to the tone of his every word,
their heads held at attentive angles,
like ministering angels?

Lying back, watching the sky, imagining shapes
the stars take on by his saying: the crab, he
says,
the bear and over there, the owl, and next to it,
some fish rising to the surface to drink the air,
and trees stirring the breeze early in the day,
like today with the sun winking, playing

each water drop caught on their leaves.

How did he ever notice his loneliness
over the sound of the animals' calm breathing,
behind their attention; his loneliness beyond
the attraction of the sky, the seductive darkness
around him, and the sound of gods walking
in the garden calling his name?

The Edge

The familiar rooms grew smaller and smaller,
the walls crushed in, the ceilings pressed down.
It seemed only natural — opening the window
stepping out on the ledge, enjoying the night —
so many-many stars, a little sliver of a moon,
the sequence of sounds the night makes:
a dog in the distance, a brief siren, a breeze,
the street, so busy all day, asleep, or going
to sleep, even the silence, he cherishes, fits,
has a place in the mix. Night surprises him

with its embrace, the way it holds him in its
cold arms, the way it sways him on the ledge,
teeters him near the edge. His foot slips a bit
but holds, waits for his choice. A voice
whispers,
welcomes him home. He stands five floors up
on a six-inch ledge, foolhardy, brave, ready to
test his wings. How could he not be able to fly?

Guy Farmer

Quiet Spaces

It's in the quiet spaces
Between words that he remembers
What he was and how it all
Led to this moment, whether
He wanted it to or not,
Without any semblance of order
Save for every single experience,
Every instance of gushing pain,
Pulsating regret, momentary joy,
And the evolving realization
That he was never whom they
Said he was, or whom he had
Convinced himself to be.

Reliving

They robbed him of
His trust, took away
His safety, denied
Him kindness, replaced
It all with harsh words
And threats of pain.
He likes to pretend
That everything's okay
But he thinks and behaves
In ways that mirror
What he went through,
Perpetuating the cycle.
It's not that he
Wants to be this way,
It's that he believes he has
No other choice,
To interrupt it would mean
Reliving the horror.

As If Nothing

Unwittingly,
Irrevocably
Steeped in a
Culture that rewards
Superficial displays of
Bluster masking
Crippling insecurity.
A child flexing its muscle,
Immersed in the language and
Lifestyle of violence,
As if nothing;
Perpetuating misery,
Dysfunction.

Shallow Blather

He doesn't ask questions
Because he's afraid
Of the answers he
Might hear.
This leaves only one option:
Talk all the time,
Fill up the space
With shallow blather.
At least this way,
He assures himself,
They won't
Be on to him.
A superficial being
Desperately trying
To avoid
Looking at itself.

A Fine Evening

A group of well-dressed,
Impeccably-coiffed
People relax in a
Posh restaurant,
Enjoying drinks and
Waiting for their order.
A light conversation
Rapidly becomes tense
When someone's feelings
Are hurt which, in turn,
Causes someone else to
Become incensed, which
Leads to someone else crying
While two others argue
In the corner and someone
Else storms out of the room
On such a fine evening.

Ian Fletcher

At a Graduation Ceremony

They inhabit a different reality
safe in the cocoon of their youthful world
like expectant passengers on a quay
about to embark on an endless cruise
their adult life a great ship that will sail
across oceans of possibility.
Alas, my ship has passed over those seas
and nears its final destination
that dark port at the end of the voyage
a place of twilight then eternal night.
Though these callow souls seem quite unaware
of the current's pull that carries all there
I'll not waste my breath to enlighten them
for of my thoughts they neither know nor care.

Man of the Suburbs

For better or for worse
like most of us I suppose
he considers himself to be
the center of the universe.
Yes, with his wife and kids
steady job, detached house
and paid-up pension scheme,
everything's absolutely fine
in his trivial suburban life
all going to plan we can see
from what he posts online.
He worships no deity
fears no kingdom come
and seems quite serene
when all is said and done
living in the here and now
his comfortable existence
sufficing for immortality.
Yet, one day this smug man
too will succumb to time

and though a few might weep
perfunctory tears for a while
at the well-attended funeral
in a generation not a soul
will remember he has gone.
Then, his only trace may be
the frozen Facebook page
on some forgotten database
where his final profile pic
will grin inanely on and on.

Breakdown

We all must have our anchors
to keep us sane, whether they be
family, friends, a job or hobby,
solid things to ground us in reality
or perhaps enable our escape from it
too much truth being dangerous
as the wise old poet once claimed.
Alas, she, she who had all of these

has slipped free of her moorings
and has sailed far out of reach
her mind adrift on stormy seas.

Poet

So you think your sage reflections
will cement your reputation
throughout the ages. Indeed,
as far as your ego is concerned
your place in posterity is guaranteed.
Yet your wise words will not save
you from the grave nor the verses
that you craft be anything more
substantial than your own epitaph.

Death in the Suburbs

It came as no surprise at all
when the old lady expired
never more to open the door
of her empty suburban home
after the two grueling months
away in the intensive care ward
her organs failing one by one.
Though he deemed it a mercy
that she had now passed on
there at the crematorium he felt
a moment or two of filial grief
with some trite reflections
on the transience of life
but was soon brought round
by his most practical wife
who if the truth be told
had never really much liked
her deceased mother-in-law.
So before a month had passed
the house of his childhood

was on sale at three hundred
and fifty thousand pounds
for life must go on he knows
his wife already pricing up
the new extension and patio.

Allison Grayhurst

Body of the Whale

Burnt, engraved
slipped for weeks walking on
a shallow incline. I could not choose
my steps or wear anything but out-worn
shoes.
I could only be this one way and pray
I was not being deceived.

After many falls and aching ankles, thumb-
joints, landing-joints,
and my tears in constant flow, I decided not
to move,
stay as a sunken root, let the mud flood
around me, driving me deeper into the
stench.

Fears like a cord tied to my feet, tugging me
down where even
undulation ceased and it was cold and
simple, without cause
or mercy or chance of escape.

I am at the bottom, somehow still myself.
There are strange translucent reptiles
brushing
at my extremities. No way to eat and no
breath left to be had,
under here in this lightless territory, not
much different
than the depths of space, than the place I was
first born.

But there, I was one with the darkness, and
the stillness of void
was tender, womb-like, all I knew. I will find
that again here,

stop resisting, diffuse, painfully, but with the least amount
of rebellion or horror - dissolve like candy floss in a child's
mouth until I join the blank weight digestive track,
welcome the bottom feeders and the algae pocket swirls
as my own flesh, until there is nothing left of me but this indent bed,
the space inside this bed that keeps my body. And soon
even that will fold over, coalesce, as though it never was.

I was a daughter. I am not anymore. I was waiting
on a personal love, rescue like a clean wave coming to
liquidate my mind. I am not waiting anymore.
I have no strength for hope, no heart

to withstand the hurt.
I break a part and I gather, honouring
the end of my pulse and its reign.

Cardinal

We walked beside the wall
on a grim February afternoon.
Our lips parted wanting to speak,
but words grazed the sound waves like
ghosts and our hearts sank.
We walked together, over logs of rotted wood,
through slush puddles, avoiding snowbanks
and icicles dangling from high trees, beside
the wall.

This is love, you told me, and I knew it to be true.
I grew tired and you linked our arms. You grew despondent

and I looked into your eyes like looking at a flower.
The winds turned on us. Family dug ditches of judgment
around us, expecting our downfall.

The cardinal arrived, leading the way, navigating
us through — stopped on a wire while we rested, called at us
to turn a corner. Around that corner, holding hands,
the wall disappeared.

Our hair damp with snow, our gloves ripped at the fingertips, we sat on a neighbourhood rock, in a yard
where nobody was home. The cardinal left when a stranger
appeared. You helped me up and we continue on

houses all around us, children going to
school, and us together
inseparable, strong in love, stronger than the
hard hard world.

Hooked

Lips pulsing, forehead
enduring — pound, pound
in the nightmare night —
high winds, blazing storm
and thinking "all alone!"
Centre of a circle, surrounded by loved ones
who have turned their backs —
poverty shame, fed-up with helping.
And there it is, the rabbit screaming
in a leg-hold trap, compressed, bones
snapped.
There is this place of Earth called home,
survival

and self-preservation paramount. Nearing now
the rotted root, my hands are slashed,
fingers twisted "Do not land!" the voice says,
pulsing as I sleep, denying all pleas for mercy.

My father would have saved me, but he is dead,
died long ago, too young of too big and too broken
a heart. My father would have helped me with love
in his eyes, growing old would not have blocked his kindness.

The streets all go south to the lake and drown
in freezing polluted waters. I go south with them,
passing beach houses, cafes I once sat at.
I am done here, let me be done, I can
not carry this inheritance.

I cannot lift my foot another step.
I have one true-heart companion and we have
been shunned together — our home, our children
taken from us to feed the snapping jaw.
Dreams made of thin glass, roses plucked to the core.
Take me like a log and feed me to the campfire, let me
turn to ash so I can start again.

Fuller Octave Frequency

Quick, the altered parable,
which once was wise words, has become
a chapel to rest in, to find a fire whistling
and dust crevices full of infant images
just starting to talk.

Quick, death is dying, the division
between houses has dissolved.

Mother is a shell, busted.
Mother is morning crashing against a bell —
chime and resound — the streets are
tempered
with your protection. Quick, the graves
have turned into sun disks, have turned again
into a vastness that is infinity that is personal
and kisses my forehead first, then my lips,
and then
knows how to purge me of my sleep.

Quick, my bones are sucked of their water,
my wealth is in my organs, pouring off my
skin
like flakes of glitter. Blow the hair from
my eyes, see me for who I am — daughter of
the egg
and animal speaker. The weight inside of me
is sheared.

I will not carry that crude responsibility
anymore. Quick,

see me off this cloud plateau, bring me down
so I can dig
with both hands into earth, my head raised,
listening
to the squirrels laugh, experiencing the joy of
a sunny day
as they twirl around a tree, three dizzy with
exuberance.

I topple over, and I am made.
You are pressed against my back and I am
holding
your hand. Quick

take my hayride, my daily routines,
dunk me in your ocean, hearing
the lyrics that arrive in a melody of pluming
intimacy.
Walking close to the sidewalk curb — death is
nothing.
You are showing me this — death is
temporary, love

is the eternal blood flow. We are all
(even the stones even the weeds)
whispering, combined.

Rodents and Wings

Days of holding up the second wall,
sustaining with syringe feedings and lifting
the broken Venetian blinds.
Days of extremes, straining to stay afloat
in a flood of despair and then given a
miracle season of joy until misfortune
overtook again.
You told me to walk, and I did. You told me
in order to heal the wound, I must first see
the wound.
You told to keep the water moving,
make waves with my hands and never stop
stroking the surface.
I loved without complaint- washed tiny toes
in the sink,

kissed a forehead, made medicine in the kitchen.
My efforts worked, for a while
until they stopped working and death had its claim.

At the exact moment of death as I watched a body
struggle to sustain breath then stop struggling,
you gave me sight to see a spirit rising,
speaking of thanks and love and vows,
showed me the ropes of attachment, strings of light
that need release before a soul can give way to illumination,
dissolve intact, no vigor or sorrow, but merging with the whole,
into the light that is blackness, that is not void
but the absorption of all colour, holy.

You showed me and still I grew angry and embittered,
at a loss for comfort, destroyed of trust.
Two days I lingered enveloped in this terrible flame,
weeping, separated from the dance. On the third day, you came again,
pointing out a passage of perfect meaning, allowing the sun
to glow and others to be stronger than me.

Crystal patterns converging. A crack muted,
a rift mended and filled, memories
and the harshness of a permanent end.
Two islands surrender to —
two secrets painted on the beach, on the backyard shed, in the inside,
giving in fully to emptiness overtaking,
as the calm begins to carve out a niche
where it can revive, return pure, all parts
tethered faithfully to the wind.

Tara Lynn Hawk

Logs Needed

In search of my
own sublime suspension
The list of things one can remake is limited
Beds
Cakes
Sand castles
Fires
I do not want to "level up"
I want to live

Check Out

Yes, as you say
I live the dream state
Self-imposed, words chosen with
careful prediction

A tumble, then a fall
A secret
How does one find the means
To tell the whole world
to just go away
Now, I wait
For the summer
The heat and the haze
To bring me to my chosen home
However brief

Green Love Poem

My bare palms
Sought the moss on the rocks and I
walked away
Without a second thought
They said I was
in love
They were wrong

Cur Non

Why learn Latin
Naked and scared
I am
For what is left to experience
The half fool in me
With no outside validation
Fob me off if you desire
Seeking the off-road
With little fuel and no map
Why not is all I have ever known

The Science of Fire

In October of 2017 Sonoma County, California experienced a firestorm that killed forty three and burned over 8400 homes and businesses.

After the fires

The science paradoxical
Drip flame torch
Scraped brown line
Wind and heat and fuel density
Sliver of dirt memento mori
And when you see me
Remember
Twisted metal, fallen oaks, ashen mortality
Where once we slept

Richard Kalfus

Finding Our Humanity

I am a Berliner of a certain age
with a history Germans
want to forget.

My best friend is both a Muslim
and a German.
Together we watch
with compassion
as Syrian refugees
find new hope
in our country.

We take pride
in this challenge,
granting safety
to a terrified people
from a merciless dictator.

Our courage makes us human again—
reminding us of a time
when we Germans forgot
our own humanity.

The Power of Touch

Touching others has profound meaning.
It shows others that you care
To share another's joy and sadness.

A teacher's touch to a troubled child.

A father reaching out to a teenage son,
discovering love for the first time.

A homeless man begging for money for food,
welcomed both my five dollar bill
and a silent touch on the shoulder.

An aging parent who no longer knows who you are,
but feels your love
through your embrace.

A call to a grieving friend at the loss of a child
receives your touch through a consoling voice.

Women no longer have the exclusive right
to touch both men and women.

Men today may hug a friend,
a sign of an enduring bond.

Medical experts all agree:
medication in tandem with a compassionate touch
can effectively help heal
physical and emotional pain.
So never forget that by touching,
you receive a gift yourself.

A young man approached me recently.
I did not recognize him,
But he knew me.
This once homeless man,
now well-dressed and smiling
took my hand to thank me:

"You helped me turn my life around."

Was it my money or my touch?

Lament of the Aging

I am old.
So I've been told
By magazines and TV commercials,
portraying perfect complexions,
Perfect hair, no bald men here.
Perfect, sculpted bodies,
ready to jog
to save the world

In a cancer run.

I am naked
So many years ago,
Standing before the army doctor
who wrote, without a word:
"This healthy 19 year old is fit to serve."

A quick glance in the mirror now
Taking note...
the wrinkled, blotchy face
The protruding stomach
The breasts I never had
The bald head of Mr. Clean
Without the muscles
of a television day.

I look around
In the community pool
At the men and women of my age
And am comforted
In a grotesque way

to be able to say

I may be one of many
Yet not the worst
Among my peers
In this our final stage.

An American Son

"Dad, you gobble up your food
Like a vulture eating his prey."
"How can I invite Tommy for dinner
when you eat like this?"
I was 13 at the time—a sensitive boy
who knew nothing of what my father
suffered at the hands of the Nazis.

Why was I kept in the dark
about the darkest chapter
In the life of a father I loved?

It was my American mother
who understood him so well.
She knew his fear
of giving voice to the past
and burdening his American son.

So he kept the years of an entire family
lost to himself.

It was years later when I learned
that by protecting me
he was protecting himself
to be able to live in the present
and not in the past

She Survived

She Survived
She survived
on a "Children's Transport"
to England.

But the memory of her mother's
panicked attempt
to pull her
from the moving train
has never left her.

And the mother?

An SS soldier
viciously shoved her
onto a cattle car
bound—she was told—
to the "East".

G. S. Katz

Coffee and Cake, Vietnam, 1966

Went to my cousin's house
He had just come home from overseas
A year in Vietnam
Spring of 1966

He went over as an officer
Having completed college and ROTC
My family and his, in the living room
Watching slides and having coffee and cake

Kind of like a travel log of a distant world
People, customs, villages and soldiers
Seemed kind of benign, not so bad
Till the blood and gore, right in our faces

Dead bodies, napalm babies, carnage

We all let out a gasp, our suburban world crashing
My cousin said he didn't know those slides were in there
But he didn't apologize, how do you excuse war?

That night left an indelible mark
I think he wanted us to witness horror
Wars are messy, life is cheap for the repressed
My young teenage eyes, stained and opened

Booths in Dark Restaurants

Booths
Dimly lit
Towards the back
For lovers
Loners
Gangsters too

Meetings
Hand holding
Gazing in your eyes
Reflection
A glass of good wine
or a whiskey or two

Deals made
Unwritten contracts signed
Booths, where people go
to escape the clutter
and noise of everyday life

A small piece of real estate
Business or pleasure
You know where to go
See you there
Eight o'clock sharp

Loner

Success

So what

Money

Comes and goes

Putting my best move on though

Your lips on mine

Attraction then wonderland

I'm home

In the zone

Reading his biography

Brings it home

Doesn't matter whose biography

Trust me on this

I sound like a used car salesman

Industrial speaks to me

Flannel blue collar melodies

Used to have a starched white shirt

Miserable living a lie

I'm a loner

You are too

Come to me
We're gonna drink some dark stout
Slow dance and drink a few shots
Home in the early dawn
These lips
They tell my story
That's all I've got
The check is in the mail
Good as gold
Yeah
Really

Being Right — a Poem about My Mom

My Mom had the most common sense of anyone I've ever known
She was right about everything, so much so, it was infuriating at times
I bucked her many times thinking I knew better

Which of course I didn't, I was no match for her
The only thing she wasn't right about
Was her need to always be right
She didn't go looking for problems to solve
Situations presented themselves and she always had the answers

Somewhere in my 50s I discovered the joy of not being right all the time
Like her, I possess great common sense
There is a burden however for always trying to be right
If you are never wrong, how do you learn from your mistakes, I asked

I'm not sure she saw my logic
Being the matriarch, being right was burned in
It's been three years since her passing
I miss her greatly and could use a few answers, right or wrong but probably right

Fruit Man on the Corner

He has a stand at the corner of my block
Fruits and Vegetables only
Twenty-four hours a day, seven days a week
Rain or shine

I call him Fruit Man
There's two of them working twelve-hour gigs
Like a nurse's shift in a hospital
But they're not, they are the Fruit Guys

In their country they could have been doctors
Accountants or Lawyers too
At the very least cable TV installers
Here they sell fruit

No complaints from these guys
A milk crate to sit on
Stoic and friendly enough
One box of strawberries or two?

Sofia Kioroglou

Treading Water

I am walking ahead and ahead
and still in the same place.
I am treading water
walking through a morass.
I think I am making progress
but I am stuck when I keep walking.

Damascus in Syria before the War

I love spring
Whenever I look out the window
I see a riot of color.

Flowers of all forms and sizes
Blossoming in my garden
after being shrinking violets.

But Nigella damascena
is my favourite, reminding me
of Damascus in Syria before the war

Reminding me that the Chaghoura,
the beautiful gazelle will protect me
from snipers, rapists and bombs

Through the Myrtle Fields

The Mediterranean sea
the blue sea par excellence
the Mare Nostrum of the Romans
the turquoise blue of us Greeks.
It soothes me and caresses me
with its gentle breeze,
wafting my mind's fog
through the myrtle fields.

Ode to Cyprus

O troubled Isle of Aphrodite
So battered by hostile winds
that vie with one another
When will this storm abate?

O thou, my father's land
Thy very heart so torn and so in pain
A castaway from thy native land
thy core is rent in twain

Strewn across thy verdant carpet
Soldiers have trampled thou like mire in the streets
O Cyprus, the lovely isle of fruitful vine
When will you breathe again?

What I Call Poetry

I know I am not much of a poet myself
I just love to describe what I see
what touches my heart, what leaps to mind.

When the words do not come out quite right
and the rhythm is a bit off-key
I don' t get my knickers in a twist

Poetry is not about the best masterpiece
but about letting my words flow like a broken dam
allowing the pen to scribble all over a blank page

Tricia Knoll

Body Language

The crows at my mailbox fear how I wave my
hallelujah hands
then hop back for their second chance at the
cat kibble I lay
down for them. Honeybees arriving at my
garden for morning's
feast seem to know — or trust — I won't hurt
them as I yank
away dry blooms of blue geraniums. They
could brandish
stinger retribution, but sharing the gold of
morning, they read
me right. At the theater, some people won't
sit next to me.
I cannot sit still. I jiggle my feet, kick my legs.
Particularly in

the second act, when the married couple
confronts how they
don't always like their kids and their kids
seem to not like them
at all. Antsy. I fidget like a flock of startled
grackles, ants on
moving day. What I can't figure is how that
kid sat through
Bible study at Emanuel AME Church and
never gave away the
gun-burden in his heart.

First printed in *Sparrow's Trill — Writers Respond to the Charleston Shooting* (Minerva Rising Literary Journal) and reprinted in Tricia Knoll's *How I Learned to Be White* (Antrim House).

The Night I Didn't Stand Up

That rock concert in New Haven took me by surprise
and why — the national anthem and the crowd was ready.
As one, the many stood and hooted for the band.

I didn't, a white girl whose knees knocked.
Angry under the videos of carpet bombing
of Cambodia, over-the-top, over-the-edge saturation
killing in Cambodia. This was my country 'tis of thee.
I sat in protest. Forty years later a quarterback kneeled
with more courage than I had in that pot-smoke crowd.
I ducked when some guy yelled I should stand.

There are times when you can't, when the wrong

is too great, and the great isn't great enough. So when
Judge Ruth says it's wrong not to stand but not illegal,
I know it can be right and the only thing you can do.
Better to let wrong drive you to your knees

than sit like a numb ass.

First published in *Social Justice Poetry* and reprinted in Tricia Knoll's *How I Learned to Be White* (Antrim House/2018).

Portland's Waterfront History

If my hometown is a Portlandia joke, it's a shaggy dog story
about a burly German Shepherd chasing Canada geese
up the waterfront. Muddy paw prints. A couple's brisk-walk chat
about gluten-free sambusas near the police memorial.

If it's an epic, then it's the lineage of birthright river people,
ten thousand gathered on these banks where geese feed now,
their fires burning below drum-talk of fish, trade and mates.
This park named for Elizabeth Caruthers, first white settler.
If a discarded history book, yellow at the edges, then it's not

the down-played flood allowed to destroy
red-lined Vanport,
but more often sepia photos of two rich white men
who flipped a coin to name a bustling
stumptown.

Today on the northernmost stone bench, I read Stafford.
Star-clusters of cherry blossoms sway
overhead, blessing
thirteen granite slabs carved with Nikkei poems. And names
of internment camps. His voice: Now is made out of ghosts.

First published in *Gyroscope Review* and then reprinted in Tricia Knoll's *How I Learned to Be White* (Antrim House, 2018).

Let's Hear It for the Horses

One million dead in the Civil War,
if you count the mules.
Which I do.

I say, blowtorch the rebel men
off their statue mounts and keep
the horses prancing on their pedestals.

They were not traitors
to their country, showed no sign
of caring who they carried,
black or white, male or
female. No one questions
their service to equality.

They did the work
they were asked to do
without a nod at glory.

First published in *New Verse News* and reprinted in her new book, *How I Learned to Be White*.

Connecting

I'm white space
between black dots.
I grew up catching tigers
by the toe. School books
came with unbroken backs.
No one ever called my people X.
Families on TV looked like mine.
I burn in the sun. I believed
money could get me where I wanted to go.

I own the land I live on.
I was never a melting anything —
fondue, chocolate, molten pot,
hot lava lamp or zombie brain.

A bubble surrounds me,
shimmer-soap surprise
I thought would never pop
until it did.

First published in *To Wake, To Rise: Meditations on Justice and Resilience* (Skinner House Books) and reprinted in Tricia Knoll's *How I Learned to Be White* (Antrim House).

Joan Leotta

Not Your Everyday Venus

I am not your everyday Venus,
emerging from the sea
unclothed, open, served up to you
on the half shell.
In fact, you see me, fully clothed
tight frilled collar banding my
graceful neck, head turned toward you,
one hand on my favorite reading chair,
the place where I escape all your
expectations.
Yet, there is more, much more to me.
But you will never know me
unless you learn
to breathe underwater, for I have not
emerged. The sea is still my home.
You see only what I am
willing to share.

Resilience

Wet,
hot
in the dark—
Puerto Rico
after Maria
Each day brings
new troubles,
breaking dams,
dire discoveries.
yet the people
greet each day's
new light
determined to
rebuild—
hope.

Pax Americana Finis

My daughter once asked
me how it was that I traveled
alone on trains through
Europe fearlessly.
I told her it was a different
time: Pax Americana was
settled over the world,
a coverlet that cosseted
us all, spread from USA
to Berlin wall,
up to the Soviet Bloc.
Within that bubble
anything was possible.
Now my confidence
is marred by tears
in the very substance of peace—
not because of terrorists.
They can kill me only once.
Rather, on this Memorial
Day, I realize all of

those who died so we
could live in peace
have been betrayed,
Our allies shake their
heads and murmur,
"America is great no more."
Pax Americana Finis

Deciding Factor

As we pulled up to the last house
late on a winter afternoon,
when they sky was already dark,
the realtor said, "This
little cottage is just right for you."
I told the realtor,
"For me, the kitchen will
decide it."
I nodded approval at the open
living room, hardwood floors,
half bath on first floor.

Then the kitchen.
Winter skies blacked two
windows above the sink,
but that was not so bad. No,
it was the muted tones, tiny
light bulb, the way the cabinets
rejected all brightness, all joy.
Food prepared here
would barely sustain the body,
let alone feed the soul.
I decided against it.

Clouds

The fence looms large
to keep me from the fields
but it cannot for
I am drawn, drawn strongly
to those clouds—
clouds of net
waving, wafting,

whispering to me
with their seductive curves
and soft almost silent sounds
as they move across the sky.
They are Dream Catchers—
large enough
so that if,
if I can reach them
these netted clouds will
hold and carry me off to my
dream world, safely caught,
not trapped,
carry me into a world
where there are no fences
between you and me.

Marie MacSweeney

The Water Bowl

Inspired by seeing the Neolithic bowl, circa 3,500 BC, discovered in a cave in Annagh, Co. Limerick.

Confluence of two rivers,
drenching chatter crushed
by howling winter
wind
so that, all their lives
thereafter,
they would deem,
his spirit a white
blizzard
floating upward
to where the cavern was,
the procession
following,

the brown-haired silent one
haughty
in her grief,
stiffly bearing
the bowl,
storm echoing within
as they entered
through scattered debris,
bones of ox, sheep,
boar and deer,
bear and wolf,

to lay him by an inner wall,
arming him for all time
with an axe,
soothing
him
as they pinned
his tunic warm across
his chest,
deer antler pillows
under his feet.

The water bowl she carried
rested on the ledge above
when it was found
six thousand years later
stretching to the edges
of our lives.

Gold Boat

Inspired by the Broighter Boat, 100 BC,
20cm long, found by the sea near Lough
Foyle, Co. Derry.

How do you
count those steps
if you are walking
on water,
if that dream boat
of gold ore ferries you
beyond a crush of seabirds
to the bare ocean

where waves surge
over you?
How do you count
your steps?

Or if the crew
is set to make music
and your feet
stumble
how will you dance
if there is not
space to place
those dancing feet?

To relish tides,
you must
abandon yourself
to rhythms
other than samba
or storm or creed
or country,
so how will your sea feet

dance?

And when the cliffs
of tall islands
hang in the distance
like curtains
calling you home
in that skin boat
which is fluent as gold,
and, though sea
yet hauls you out

how will you dance?

The Flint Napper

Inspired by the Flint Macehead, 3300/2800 BC, found at Knowth, Co. Meath.

And if he dreams,
how now does he dream

in winter dark,
of the finished work,
of the flint when he first
saw it, as he rinsed it in the river,
or the lure of its pale grey
significance, patched with brown?

And if he dreams now
is it of wrestling the stone
into a head, chipping
excess flakes away,
or of the elegant spirals
he shaped, hand skipping across hand
until he closed over the edges
into ears and eyes?

The brown forehead
is decorated with lozenges,
the mouth a howling war
that may not ease
until the shaft
stabs through.

Is this then the dream,
or a nightmare,
the warrior mace in his King's hands,
a battle, the anguished ascent
to the cairn on the hill,
the royal burial urn?

Carrier Bag

Inspired by the Neolithic bag, 3800 BC to
2500, BC, found in a bog in Twyford, Co.
Westmeath.

Blackberries, sloes, hazel nuts
at the bottom of this bag.
Occasional fraughans too,
and sour wild apples.
Always the child by her side
during these excursions,
though not productive,
preferring to flirt with her reflection

in the lake, a specious alchemy
and not to be trusted.

Earlier she had assembled the bag,
gouging slivers of wood
from saplings, coiling them
around a central core, a satisfaction
in each curve as the wind swayed
and starlings flickered overhead.

She may have waited
until the dye seeped
into each cell
before adding grass,
sitting by a winter fire,
sepia land swollen with cold;
and the handle came in spring,
before they set out again
to forage, cabbage, water cress,
wild lettuce.

Six thousand years later

I call to mind my first bag,
crisp cotton stiffened with
cardboard, an entire world
inside there as I went out,
a scrap of her reticence
lodged in my heart,
the newness of things,
stability and fragility,
the way we will
never know more than part
of what there is.

Gold Hoard

Inspired by the Mooghaun Hoard. Circa 800 BC, found near Newmarket-on-Fergus, Co. Clare.

See the plunge of gold
into their pockets
and petticoats,

bracelets pressing
hard against flesh,
collars and torcs
awkward weights
hung from many waists,
the startled infant in her shawl
hurt by the surprise of it all;

see how in retreat,
they buried all in haste,
enclosed their find with rocks
and shingle, all gone from them
but the bracelet thrust
next to the infant's heart.

Millennia later the labourer
unearthing the hoard
has a flash dream in which he drapes
his sepia wife in robes of gold,
takes her to a fancy dance,
stretches them both a little larger
than their lives,

and lingers there
until the broad estuary
is sucked out to sea,
gulls tumbling low
over a restless Shannon.

Carolyn Martin

Along the Desert View Trail on Mount San Jacinto

Palm Springs, California

Maybe it was the wind at 8500 feet
or my sneakers navigating slushy snow
or the cloudless sun that kept the chill at bay.

Maybe it was the Western gray —
the wildest squirrel to cross our paths —
on her midden trail. Or spalls of rock

spilling down mountainsides. Or hikers
dropping packs to share their lives.
Maybe it was nothing more than my mind

insisting that close-ups concentrate,
panoramas amaze. No matter why,

persistent words echoed every turn:

Stop to notice and you're saved.
A shooting star in seven syllables,
an epigram designed to stall my pace.

Of course attention must be paid —
for astonishment and memories
and photographs bound for my next book —

and I'm adept at paying on the spot.
It's the second thought that stumped.
I didn't know I needed to be saved.

From what — or for? I ask the melting path.
The dinge of earth with all its reckless noise?
The awe-filled grace of clarity? Vistas
missed?

Maybe answers hide in crevices
where lizards sleep or in nests built high
above a bobcat's reach. I'll turn those words

slowly in my hand, then bounce them
off the canyon's walls. Some sense may echo
back before they dismay again.

Tourists at Re-Mudding Time

San Francisco de Asis Mission Church
Rancho de Taos, New Mexico

Small doses of morning shade
and we stand where Adams and O'Keefe
used to set up shop. Today, the beat
of tribal rock and smells of roses, straw,
and dust as a band of citizens
scrapes adobe off the mission's walls.

The Spanish priest, suave and self-assured
in white-collared black, wanders by
and shows us how Taos temperatures crack
tamped-earth buttresses and why each June
community and mud restore their strength.

Then, without a pause, he launches into
stories of pueblo lands soaked in blood,
tribes who turned each other into slaves,
Penitentes who flagellate themselves.
He holds us in the palm of his words
until he says, Carson is a dirty name
and Natives wallow in their victimhood.

Stunned and confused, we're tempted to protest,
What about Inquisitors? Jesuits?
Conquistadors? but we hold back.

Driving north, we wonder who designed
all those take-for-granted tales encircling
mountain men, the cavalry, and Navajos?
Who decides catastrophes are victories?
We've yet to understand all we need to learn
as we pass Kit Carson Drive, Museum,
Park, and resting place in the almost-dark.

A Requiem in November

They hadn't given up. Last night they thumbed
their stems at nasty wind and rain
and scooted south to hide in soggy grass.

This morning they held their colors fast,
clinging to gloves, boots, and rakes, begging for
a stab at life for another day.

What do you do when sugar maples' reds
and yellow-oranges make you want to cry?
When short-lived intensity asks for help?

You could decoupage the yard, then melt
blocks of paraffin and dip hangers-on
on every lichened limb. You could explain

it's nothing personal. Point out basil,
begonias, coleus ripped by frost.

You could concede that Nature is unkind

when your valley's snow rarely falls below
five hundred feet and nothing you prescribe
can relieve months of gray. A last resort,

you could rake a pyre and jump spread-
eagled
into its multi-colored heart, bearing
witness to each leaf as it crisps and fades.

One Does as One Must

"One does as one must."
— Robert Draper, "Lifeblood,"
National Geographic, October 2015.

Tonight I was starting to complain
about my scratchy sheets
when I recalled the photograph.
Not the one where young ship-breakers

in Bangladesh sleep in soot and despair
beneath sheets of unhinged steel.

Nor the one where Filipino men sleep
eight to a room in the furnace of Dubai.
Eight bodies scarred from welding steel,
bedded down in shifts to save on rent.
Eight families far away waiting
for their remittance checks.

Tonight it's those exhausted eyes bedded
on burlap sacks on the Congo's waterway.
The journalist explains that shysters steal
eighty bucks a head to drift for months
in starts and stops. The overloaded barge
floats on bribes and a chugging engine's
cough.

Harvesters, prostitutes, cooks,
hope-seeking families — so tired
they can't recall where they've been
or where they believed they'd land. I wonder,

as I pull my covers up, if they dream
about the night they'll die on a breathless deck,
or the hour strangers will wrap their lives
in dirty sheets after they float to shore.

Elusive

... the words for what I ate last night
as dinner progressed and friends probed
why I didn't call when the stove top flamed
and the sump pump failed. I couldn't bring myself
to explain their numbers frozen in a cell
resting on an ice cube tray.

And here's more perplexity:
My long-term storage space overflows
with grade-school shame, teenage taunts,
resentments, blame tucked behind
photographs

of my first love and snips of poems, hymns,
and prayers. As they escape, I confuse
the where and when of everything.

Yet there's relief on mornings
when my coffee almost tastes the way it
should
and the neighbor's gray-striped cat shows up
to see if I'm still here. She doesn't seem
to mind I can't recall last night's Good Wife
or make a dozen empty trips from room to
room.
I offer her a nod and whisper words only
she can hear. Something about a poem
I wrote and can't find anywhere.

Previously published in *The Galway Review*.

Diane G. Martin

Summer Gardens

And still Medusa guards the gardens
from attack by other mortals,
her androgynous, bronze, hideous
face sweating ire from open pores till

wet, half-hearted snowflakes spit at
it. Her snakes uncoil, a wrathful,
silent, rising... dumb, unseen, by
children, lovers, drunks, whose path full

of white, twilit purpose, slide,
mumble, stumble round the swanless
pond, forgetting the threat growing
at the gates. The Gorgon, harmless

mortal sister, has fenced us in.
Snakes slither out terrified, wide

eyes, shocked, gaping mouth... entwine sharp,
iron stakes, and bind, squeeze us hard.

Morning finds more marble statues.
Blind.

March 2017
St. Petersburg, Russia

Nursery Rhyme

Wife Spratt is too fat,
her husband, too thin.
Within historic ramparts,
it's the way of things,
though clamoring beggars
make such a din.

A refugee serves her.
Has she heard that children

are practice targets there?
She refuses to hear
in this bar or anywhere.

Why spoil the sunset?
She'll regret her visit.
See her great new shoes instead.
Aren't they exquisite?

Home again, home again,
jiggety jig.
On the taxi radio,
a tiresome interview:

Q: A small window of opportunity?

A: Yes, while it's a terrible thing to say
    that an outbreak of polio
    can offer us hope in these dark ages
    of chemical weapons and religious
    rages, an epidemic is in no
    one's interest across the region.

Q: What's the humanitarian lesson?

Her shoes begin to pinch,
so Wife asks Husband Spratt
about giving an inch.
It's naïve to support
bad economics
by shedding your tears,
he assures. Asylum
is costly, my dear.
Turn on the fairy lights,
come here and bring me a beer.

November 2013
Sansepolcro, Italy

Over the Yardarm

The balloon man bicycles past
the super yachts
and the man with the prosthesis,
handsome, though losing his teeth.

He's been put with a bowl to beg
since losing his leg.
I don't know how he gets by with
the price of coffin nails what it is.

Come here from Aydin for the tourist
season, I've learned.
We shared a bench and a sunset,
though no exchange but geography

and pantomime. Shadow puppets both.

April 22, 2014
Bodrum, Turkey

Winterreise

"Shall I join you on your journey?
Will you play the music to my song?"
— Müller/Schubert, "The Hurdy Gurdy Man"

No fires or chestnut vendors
grace the shadowed streets, just
shivering, bared hookers,
bored, staked out on their pitches,

glittering spike heels and
cigarettes their only weapons,
lit toward the tilting johns
in blackened corners.

A deeply lined Turk mourns
his move and mine with his
duduk. So, sister, can you
spare a dime? Is it time?

Winter wind jabs, probes soft patches

of exposed flesh, piercing it
with a sharp blade beneath my
Lithuanian coat, buttons

dangling, holes much mended.
My Estonian hand-crafted
hat, crushed, brim bent, tips threads of
embroidered jet beads down,

unravelling remembrance,
sadder than a broken chord.
A brightly lighted train streaks
overhead and my split-zippered

Finnish boots trip, stumble
into curbside puddles,
seeping through my socks like wet
rejection notices.

Relentless thump of canned pop
blares, heart jarring through half-
hearted snow that fails to stick.

Berlin's bleak winter's stillborn

 in D minor. Drunks accost
me mildly, aiming one word,
"MAMA" like a crooked dart.
And a "Je suis Charlie" hat smiles.

February 16, 2015
Berlin, Germany

Remembrance for Rosemary

For R. Kennedy.

Rosemary, how far did you get
into the Lord's Prayer before
the butter knife sliced away its
meter, bit into its meat? Wry

supplicant that you were, willful,
playful, lustful no more. Your trust

in fathers, thoroughly misplaced,
supplied the big men with grim grist

for their mills, you hence, only stone.
Did they lament at all—Doctor,
Daddy—the experiment gone
wrong, or smashing the oath to do

no harm?

June 2016
Gümüslük, Turkey

Stan Morrison

What If

What if I had just stayed in New York?
What if Abraham dared to eat pork?
Binary systems give us only either/or
Parallel universes offer so much more

What if Columbus had just turned around?
What if Newton's apple didn't hit the ground?
Nothing really defies imagination
Just consider all the permutations

What if frogs had fur on their backs?
What if moose never left any tracks?
There're more possibilities between heaven and earth
From the house of gloom to the house of mirth

What if salmon only swam downstream?
What if things weren't always as they seem?
Children should be seen and not heard
Excellent advice for the totally absurd!

Drumbeat

I want
I need
But life doesn't
Last that long
I was thinking
I was planning
But life doesn't
Last that long
I was wondering
I was hoping
But life doesn't

Swamp People

Somethin' weird is goin' on
And I think that I know why
The Milk of Human Kindness
Is substituted by somethin' sour
The needs of the overfed
Trump those of the underweight
They don't need no education
They just need mind control

Death at an Early Age

Fathers, brothers and uncles
Abuse little boys and girls
Unrepentant criminals
Murder these tiny souls

Murder looks like suicide
For our brothers and sisters
Death of innocence

Betrayal of trust
Death of childhood
End of self-worth

The remorseless predators
Have perfected their craft
Victims visit their therapists
While the doers shrug it off

Abusers are protected by
The silence of the victims
The enabling witnesses
Ignoring the so obvious

Rapists seek out more victims
Starting young so they'll obey
Perverted thrills are re-ignited
The casualties of human nature.

Politics and the English Language

A lifetime of public service
Is but an impenetrable surfeit
For fame and respectability
For access to public funds
An endless supply of bribes
A war chest for re-election
A plausible cover-up for crimes
Some fraction of the people
Eternally grateful/uninformed
Blindly follows despite evidence
"Some folks rob you with a six-gun
Others with a fountain pen."

Bonnie Burka Shannon

The Numbers Game

I must accept
That I was never
Number one

Even before
There were others
In the mix
I was not destined
To be number one

Even before
I was hatched
I was not meant
To be anyone's true
Pride and joy
Number one
Means you are

The epicenter
Of someone's universe
What feat must one achieve
To be another's
Center of the world

Some achieve that
Before they are born
And I
Am envious

He Never Expresses Regret

The child will never recover
From you
But life goes on
Doesn't it

Even though
They shoot horses
Don't they

Life endures
In a manner
That is hard
To label

You have destroyed
What she believed in
You have policed her life
And the lives
Of others

You tell untruths
Fabricate
Deflect
Blame
Retract and restate

You require
Complete allegiance
While most
Never believed
Or were all deceived

You typify a
Borderline Personality
Not so complicated
After all
Just malevolent
Immoral
And self-absorbed
A true narcissist

You have devastated
What she once
Had faith in
You have regulated her vitality
Tarnished her convictions
Unfastened her life
And the lives
Of others

And you never
Express regret
Or shame

A Need to Travel

I am at a loss
I thought
We had
An understanding
But you did it
Again

The troubling episodes
Always occur
Out of nowhere
Just when I have grown
To feel comfortable
And safe with you
Once more

What causes
This transformation
In you
Who in your history
Made you feel

So inadequate

Perhaps I will
Never know
Or understand
The roots of
Your psychology
Your demons

But I am weary
So weary
Of this thing
This behavior
That alters
Who I once thought
You to be

I move far away
Physically
And emotionally
As if I have relocated
To another planet

Someday
I may travel
So far away
That I cannot
Will not
Resurface
Perhaps
Sooner than
I imagine
Is possible

The Actress

Bereft
No funeral
In the forecast
Just the loss

The lump
In the throat
A constant companion

For too long

No neediness apparent
Weakness hidden
In mirthless eyes

Damage done
Escapes made
Life goes on
They say

Life goes on

Endings

My mother died one day
We expected it
She lived longer
Than she wanted
She was ready
So were we

She told us
She did not care
What would happen
After her death
Who would be hurt
What would be destroyed

She did not care
Declaring that her offspring
Could fight it out
Because she'd be gone
And unaware

I could not pray for her
I cannot still
Yet she was
My mother

I suppose
In her own way
She loved us
But as Tina Turner

Once sang,
What's love
Got to do
With it

We were all damaged
Still are
And yet
Sometimes I
Pick up the phone
To call her
And remember

What was she thinking
The moment
When she died
I will never know
Funny thing is
I miss her

Langley Shazor

Shards of Glass

What is it
What am I so desperately searching for
Smiles
Thumbs up
Hearts
Numbers
Every spare moment spent
Glued to bright screens
Counting and analyzing
Is it approval
Do I need strangers and acquaintances
Friends and family
To leave evidence
Vividly adorned proof
That I may feel better about myself
I justify this constant updating
Colloquially

However
Is it a means to an end
Some vehicle to ascension
A vector for success
Is this not success currently
Perhaps
I am simply as obsessed
And as vain
An air of narcissism
Combusted
By a flame of loneliness
Striving to be on par
All these virtual competitors
Vying for a piece
Of this digital pie
Am I truly a revolutionary
Or a pseudo unplugging opportunist
Harboring the same programmed
Involuntary
Identity crisis

Predilections

Postulation
The presence of exception
Being the catalyst
For circumventing
Rules and regulations
To usurp authority
Paving bold pathways
Uncharted
Precipitous

Ergo adrenaline
Forces cerebrums to capitulate
Shattered barriers
Materialize into the natural order
Human condition
Builds success
Upon a succession of destruction
Thus
We continue perpetuating
Temporary boundaries

Hand Crafted

I haven't

Written

In a while

That's what I tell

Myself

And everyone else

Keeping motivation

At the forefront

This lobe

Conjuring electrical

Involuntary impulses

Resulting incoherent

Ramblings

Restructured

Reorganized

Transferring down limbs

Kinetic potential

Manifest metacarpal motion

Furious phalangetic freedom

Forever finds phrases to frisk

Across open spaces
And frolic they must
Expend this energy
Pent up power
Because
I haven't written
Not in a while

Paper Cuts

Pardon the way this ink flows
Through keys
Through pens
From fingers and minds
Hemingway confirmed it
This blank page
Acts as an anticoagulant
Dripping from tips
Spilling over fine points
Aided by gravity
Pulsing out of open pores

A heart under attack
Remedied by these gaping slits
The pain is part of the pleasure
Drifting away
The state of euphoria
Gallops to an unfathomable high
Until the pressure is relieved
Not a single
Drop
Remains

Cosmos

Our cosmic connection
Though powerful
Falls victim to strain
During long stints
Without being recharged
With external centrifugal forces
Attempting to sling us into the universe
This electromagnetic orbit

Counters

Mitigates

A celestial tug-of-war

Mapped by ellipses

Allowing us to never travel

Too far from line of sight

Before gravitons collide

Once again

Bringing these planetary bodies

Back into alignment

Sravani Singampalli

Life Is a Glass of Coke

I sit with a glass of Coke
I take small sips
And enjoy its refreshing taste.
Conversations with my friends press on
And after some time
When I start taking another sip
It no longer tastes refreshing
No longer like Coke
But like a tea decoction.

100 Opinions and Choices

They say that red
Is the colour of 'anger'.
Why do they say this?
Red is also the colour

Of the friendly ladybird
In my garden.
Do you feel that love
Is the most intriguing thing?
Why not?
See how that old train carriage
Is being used as a bridge.
A delicacy made of chocolates
And strawberries is everybody's favourite.
Who eats a delicacy made of
Chicken eggs boiled for a whole day
In the urine of young boys?
Some Chinese do.
Butterscotch ice cream is very scrumptious.
They also sell the special
Green pea flavoured ice cream.
That little boy likes it.

Fortune cookies have lost fortune.
Now, the Geese are also
Used in night patrols
To catch the robbers.

Artificial eggs
Simultaneously occurring sunset and eclipse
A snake with two heads
So many queer things exist.
We call them 'intriguing'.
They call this poor girl
Good-for-nothing and opinionated.
I say, what were they
All these years?

The Coke lost its effervescence
Just like our extended conversations
Just like our cheeks and skin
Just like our behaviour.
The conversations become meaningless
Skin loses its elasticity
And we become forlorn citizens.

Summer 2011

I sit alone on the partially wet grass
On a hot summer day
Enveloped in silence.
I don't think about anything.
I can feel the sweat
Trickling down my back.
My sweat has a vinegary and acidic smell.
Doctors say that the bacteria
Living on my skin
Are responsible for it.
What can I do?
I bath twice a day
To feel better.
People have been harsh to me.
At times I feel isolated
But the fishes in a nearby pond
Brighten up my face.
Perhaps I was a fish
In my previous birth.
On the opposite side of the road

I behold a tree
Facing the fresh water river
On one side
And piles of garbage
On the other.

Unaware

An intense cyclone has hit a city
Heavy downpours, floods and
Loss of lives
All come in bonus.
Trees have fallen down and
Birds have lost their home.
Somewhere in another city
My friend prays for the safety
Of her relatives
After watching the news
On the television and
I stare at her from my window
Unaware of the danger

Unaware of the loss
Unaware of those lost birds.
I drink a glass of warm milk
Mixed with my favourite chocolate syrup
And go to bed as usual.
In the morning
As I open my eyes here
Many have closed their eyes there forever.
I complain of being unlucky
After my mother wakes me up so early
Unaware of my fate
Unaware of how fortunate I am.

Mind and Body

They say that his blood stinks.
His red blood cells are rotting away
Because of his misdeeds and
White blood cells have refused
To fight for him.
He knows that he was wrong that day.

He knew the repercussions.
Today those poor people have lost homes
Their children can't go to school
Just because of him.
Now, their hunger has cursed him.
His body is slowly deteriorating.
He asks for forgiveness
But some leaves
Have already wilted.

Chloe Thompson

Willow Widow

Willows sigh as I pass by,
Bones creaking in the wind.
Alone. Birds are to trees
As lice are to me.

How old am I? Shame on you.
Cut of my leg
And count the rings.
The only reliable method.

It is hard to imagine
A sturdy oak
Branch to root riddled
With wrinkles was once a sapling.

Wind and rain,
Worn my defences.

Centuries of pain,
Engraved in my bark.

Willows sigh as I pass by,
Again. To sit by my love,
Dry eyed.
He couldn't stand weeping widows.

Dark Horse

The night mare came
A thumping. Relentless heels
Carving out my deepest
Fear

Walking through the hunted
Field I feel the stench of decay
Clog my nose, my heart
Stops beating, racing. I have

Already lost. Zero horse power.

A steady stream of dead
Dream animals lay, I follow
them as I always do.
Impossible creatures,

Too fantastical, all for show
With useless fifth legs,
Rainbow wings and spiky shells
Thick as paper.

The night mare came
A striding. Top speed,
Whipping a snake-
Infested mane.

I cannot outrun it,
I cannot face it,
I cannot understand it.

Patchwork Guilt

The mind is like a patch
work quilt, growing every day.
A sacred place, your head to lay
a dream ready to hatch.

Soft silk dreams laced
with nightmares, thinly
veiled common cares
snapping at the seams.

Each patch unique,
continuous thread
of memories that even
Hercules cannot pull apart
the gorgon, lurking
in the corner. A collage
of neglected, frayed silk
and stained cotton

prone to snagging, unravelling

at night, the sheet unfolds,
spanning the country
side. Fields of different textures
shapes; filled with sheep

of the deepest red, cotton
candy pink and baby blue
sky turns a marvellous hue
of colours long forgotten.

It can only be described
as similar to the colour
of your mother's dress.

Origami birds float
overhead, raining
quotes of all the books
you have ever read.

A world of comforting,
harboring memories
of happiness, joy, glee,

loneliness and longing

to reach the end
of the pattern.
Hands ripped and tattered,
overdue a mend.

So suddenly, the dream
is gone. Awake a few
scraps remain, askew
patches that seem

incorporeal
compared to the original quilt.
Misrembered with guilt and
a single tear.

No Story

A poem once said that
Before one is dead,
They must choose
A path;

Two generation-old maps
Threaten to leave
in the harsh breeze.

Mother's map, barely used.
On the back, centuries-
Old Shopping and unchecked
Bucket lists.

The other, falling apart
With dog-eared folds, grime
Dark black grease stains.

I haven't the time
To travel both.

A choice must be made
In my prime.

On the right, faded and worn
by those who trod before,
the straight path

standard green grass
no twists
no turns or
shortcuts.

To my left, shaded and torn
Shy neglected fences,
Distant divergent paths
Barely seen above weeds.

Unsure, I feel
The pressure of poking
Impatient children
Not yet born.

One road will add
Around 20 years
To my destination

The other cuts my jour-
Ney, but
The path is mottled
With rotten leaves.

Fables, those too fast
Finish last,
Haunt me.

If red riding hood had not
Strayed from the path
(and followed mother's advice)
There would have been

No story
I think
As I walk between them.

Captivating

The sunrise caught
on film, a dim
black and white copy
compared with
the surge of red,
orange, pink, something
you can't remember
constantly changing, glooping
like a lava lamp, leaking
out of your camera.

Dead as a captive
Great White.

Niamh Twomey

Someday

Someday
I'll have my own house.

With a shelf of poetry books
By the toilet
And short stories
For those long, difficult stays.

With vibrant colours
Painted on the walls
Every wall a different colour
Like Lego.

With a deep couch
That swallows bums
And snoozing cat
Meditating on a warm fire.

With an old phone
Waiting to sing
Its wire in tangled ringlets
Coiled like angel's hair.

With oriental spices
And a box of perfumed teas
Of every fruit and flower
And porridge.

With a kettle always brooding
On the blistering hob
While friends take seats and I ask
Do you like macaroons?

With an old dusted piano
Out of tune but crooning still
Rubbed down with old underwear
Draped with a doily.

With space to move mountains
In idle passing thoughts

With sun waking rooms
Through velvet curtains in the morning.

There will be space for two heads
On the cushions on my bed
And my rusting doorbell
Will wait there for your touch,

When someday
I have my own house.

Face

I walked out of the cubicle—
A diabolical state.
I washed my hands and dried them quickly
While the girl beside me
Stared at the mirror,
Twisting the pearls on her ears
And tenderly treating her face
Like a butterfly's wing.

I watched in wonder;
Like a matted clump of seaweed
Beside a deep-sea shell.
The hand-dryer hushed.
A diabolical mess still, I walked away.
That's not how I wanted to spend my day.

Curls

After You Died
You became Enormous.
A stone in every step;
Tinnitus. Garlic-breath.
Suddenly from every spot
Bloomed a memory,
And you lived
A hundred times over
In every head
Of cinnamon curls
I saw from behind.

Sometimes I followed
Your bouncing curls down the street,
Standing back,
Willing the head not to turn
And show the face of someone else
So you would die again.

First Memory

We're going for a drive.
Dad comes home for a weekend once a month
So I'm excited.

Swallowed up in a winter coat
The world is so big.
Keys clink in Dad's giant hands.

Our Indian neighbors appear
In their driveway
We say hello and mention the weather.

Then the car door opens for me
Like a monster yawning,
I clamber upwards, fumbling for my car seat.

Maybe he will offer me a mint
From the treasury of the glove-box—
Mom never gives me mints.

As we drive away
The house with the white door
Shrinks into the estate.

And Dad spies something
Beginning with
D.

She Remembers

She remembers
Left Hand being smacked
Until Right Hand, quivering,

Picked up the pen and battled with an 'F'.

She remembers
Ten in a bed
And twelve in a car,
If they had one,
And white knuckles clutching
Her mother's skirts
In the post office.

She remembers
Eating every part of the pig,
And washing in the cold
Stream.

She remembers when colourful caravans
Came to the door,
And men with earthy smiles
And black matted manes
Melted down old pots and pans.

She remembers young lads

Joining the priesthood, not for the love of god,
But because there was nothing for them
To inherit.

She remembers the first time she saw
A banana.

She remembers walking home
With Paddy down the road
And her nattering the whole way
And him not saying a word.

She remembers marrying him
In a pink dress in September.

She remembers London in the sixties.

She remembers Roaches Stores
And condoms being legalized.

She remembers sunshine

On her flowers in the summer,
And taking slips from neighbors' gardens.

She remembers sprinklings
Of poems she learnt at school;
"Come away, O human child!
To the waters and the wild
With a faery, hand in hand,
For the world's more full of weeping—
Who wrote that again?"

POET BIOGRAPHIES

A CONTEMPORARY POETRY ANTHOLOGY

Wanda Morrow Clevenger

Wanda Morrow Clevenger is a Carlinville, IL native living in Hettick, IL. Over 500 pieces of her work appear in 162 print and electronic journals and anthologies. The first of a 5-volume chapbook series *Young and Unadorned — Where the Hogs Ate the Cabbage Volume 1* is available through Writing Knights Press.

Gareth Culshaw

Gareth lives in Wales. He published his first poetry collection with *FutureCycle* in 2018 and his work has appeared in various online and print publications across the UK and USA.

Steve Denehan

Steve Denehan lives in Kildare, Ireland with his wife Eimear and daughter Robin. He has been published in *The First Literary Review*, *Poems and Poetry*, *Third Wednesday*, *Sky Island Journal,* and *The Poet Community*.

Naduni Dineisha

I am a poet and a short story writer from Sri Lanka. My passion is living as close to nature as possible. I have a degree in English from the University of Kelaniya and I'm eager to start an academic career.

Diane Woodwad Dorff

Born in East St. Louis, Illinois, Diane Woodwad Dorff currently makes her home in Minneapolis, Minnesota. She has worked as a technical writer in the computer industry, but her first love has always been poetry. Her work has appeared in *Social Justice Poetry*, *The Poet Community*, *Hello Poetry*, *PoetrySoup*, *Haikuniverse*, and at buhlplanetarium.tripod.com/poetry/dorffd.

Robin Wyatt Dunn

Robin Wyatt Dunn writes and teaches in Los Angeles, but is trying to escape.

J. K. Durick

J. K. Durick is a writing teacher at the Community College of Vermont and an online writing tutor. His recent poems have appeared in *Social Justice Poetry*, *1947*, *Poetry Superhighway*, *Synchronized Chaos*, and *Algebra of Owls*.

Guy Farmer

Guy Farmer's poetry examines people's frailties, foibles, and triumphs and how they interact with themselves and others. He enjoys exploring hurt and brokenness, not to dwell in it, but because he believes human beings have the innate ability to heal and build a more compassionate world. Visit him online at www.unconventionalbeing.com.

Ian Fletcher

Born and raised in Cardiff, Wales, Ian has an MA in English from Oxford University. He lives in Taiwan with his wife, two daughters and cat. He teaches English in a high school. He has had poems and short stories published in *Tuck Magazine, The Ekphrastic Review, Literary Yard, 1947 A Literary Journal, Spillwords Press, The Drabble, Dead Snakes, Your One Phone Call, Schlock! Webzine, Short-story.me, Anotherealm, Under the Bed, A Story in 100 Words, Poems and Poetry, Friday Flash Fiction*, and in various anthologies.

Allison Grayhurst

Allison Grayhurst is a member of the League of Canadian Poets. Four times nominated for "Best of the Net", 2015/2017, she has over 1125 poems published in over 450 international journals and anthologies. She has 21 published books of poetry, six collections and six chapbooks. She lives in Toronto with her family. She is a vegan. She also sculpts, working with clay. Visit her online at www.allisongrayhurst.com.

Tara Lynn Hawk

Tara Lynn Hawk is the author of poetry chapbooks *Rhetorical Wanderlust* and *The Dead*. Her work is forthcoming in *Moonchild* and has appeared in *Occulum, Rasputin, Anti-Heroin Chic, Uut, The Cabinet of Heed, Spelk, Midnight Lane Gallery, The Poet Community, Idle Ink, Spilling Cocoa, Poethead, Poems and Poetry, Social Justice Poetry* and more. Visit her online at taralynnhawk.com.

Richard Kalfus

Richard Kalfus is a professor of Holocaust/Genocide Studies, a published author and award-winning educator.

G. S. Katz

The more I write what is referred to as poetry, the less I see my work that way. Although in poem format, I consider what I write to be human narratives encompassing theories of love, work, connection and spirit. Writing came late to me in life but I'm glad it did. My words define me for better or for worse.

Sofia Kioroglou

Sofia Kioroglou is an author, poet and translator from Athens, Greece. She views writing as a form of catharsis and a compass for her journey in this lifetime. Her poetry oozes youthful idealism transmuted into a conscious effort to transcend physical boundaries. Her poetry has won a number of awards and nominations both in her hometown and overseas. Visit her online at sofiakioroglou.wordpress.com.

Tricia Knoll

Tricia Knoll is an Oregon poet who got serious about writing poetry after many years of doing communications work for the City of Portland. Her poetry ranges from lyric to narrative with injections of lots of eco-poetry and poetry of political resistance. She is increasingly attracted to Zen Buddhism and confesses to having a great love for her rose garden which she never sprays. She maintains a daily haiku practice, compilations of which she gives as a holiday gift to her husband. Visit her online at triciaknoll.com.

Joan Leotta

Joan Leotta, a Pittsburgh native, is an author and story performer. Her books include, *Giulia Goes to War*, *Book One of the Legacy of Honor Series*, *Tales Through Time: Women of the South*, and *The Shenandoah Valley Book: A Complete Guide.* She writes fiction, non-fiction (food, travel, profiles) and poetry and enjoys life with her husband in Calabash, North Carolina. Visit her online at joanleotta.wordpress.com.

Marie MacSweeney

Always in love with words, Marie MacSweeney now writes poetry and short stories and has contributed to the historical journals of the Irish counties Meath and Kerry. She had two radio plays produced by Radio Telefís Eireann. Published in several anthologies, she is a winner of many awards including the Francis MacManus Award, the Phizzfest Poetry Award, Kells Poetry Award and the David Burland Award. Published also in *Irish Short Stories* (Ed. David Marcus), *Here's Me Bus* (New York), *Fortnight*, *Sunday Tribune* and *STET*. She had two poetry chapbooks published, a collection of short stories and a current affairs volume. She also featured on the radio programme, Sunday Miscellany, on numerous occasions. Visit her online at mariemacsweeney.com.

Carolyn Martin

From Assistant Professor of English to management trainer to retiree, Carolyn Martin has journeyed from New Jersey to Oregon to discover Douglas firs, months of rain, and dry summers. Her poems and book reviews have appeared in publications throughout North America and the UK, and her third poetry collection, *Thin Places*, was released by Kelsay Books in 2017.

Diane G. Martin

American photographer, poet and prose writer, Diane G. Martin, Russian literature specialist and Willamette University graduate, has published work in *New London Writers, Vine Leaves Literary Review, Poetry Circle, Open: Journal of Arts and Letters, Breath and Shadow, The Willamette Review of the Liberal Arts, Portland Review of Art, Pentimento, Twisted Vine Leaves, The Examined Life, Wordgathering, Dodging the Rain, Antiphon, Dark Ink,* and upcoming in *Gyroscope, Poor Yorick,* and *Rhino,* with photos in *Conclave, Slipstream, Dodging the Rain, Stonecoast Review,* and *Dark Ink.*

Stan Morrison

Stan Morrison is a father, grandfather, board certified pediatrician, former faculty member of Columbia University College of Physicians and Surgeons, and is currently practicing at Community Medical Centers, Lodi, CA.

Bonnie Burka Shannon

I have written poetry for most of my life. My poems are how I express my feelings — whether I am sad, happy, angry, or frustrated. My poems are about love, relationships, our nation, and people who mean a great deal to me. Some reflect issues and the emotions of those I love. I have a license in Marriage and Family Therapy and master's degrees in Reading/Special Education and School Psychology as well as a Ph.D. in Counseling Psychology.

Langley Shazor

Langley is an advocate for the performing arts, education, community involvement, and sustainable economic development. He is passionate about learning, breaking down stereotypes, creating social awareness, enlightenment, human rights, and helping those less fortunate. Langley is strongly committed to empowering today's youth and encouraging their interest in the arts. A lover of things antiquated, he is an avid typewriter collector and user who has been able to bring a forgotten medium back to life and give it relevance in this ever-growing digital world. He lives in lives in Bristol, VA.

Sravani Singampalli

Sravani Singampalli is a published writer and poet from India. Her works have appeared in *Scarlet Leaf Review, Leaves of Ink, Criterion, Setu, Whispers, Labyrinthine Passages, Indian Ruminations* and many others. Her poems are also forthcoming in *Kitaab, Formercactus, Gone Lawn, Vox Poetica, The Pangolin Review, Tuck Magazine* and elsewhere. She is presently pursuing a doctorate of pharmacy at JNTU Kakinada University in Andhra Pradesh, India.

Chloe Thompson

Chloe Thompson is a 21 year old English student currently studying at Ulster University Coleraine campus. She has no previous published work, but is an aspiring writer.

Niamh Twomey

Niamh Twomey is an Irish writer, and student of English Literature and French at the University of Cork. Since her first success as winner of Hotpress' 'Write Here Write Now' young writers competition in 2016, her work has been published in journals such as *Quill & Parchment*, *Flight Writing*, *Ink Sweat and Tears* and Cork's *Quarryman*, among others.

ALONG THE WAY

A CONTEMPORARY POETRY ANTHOLOGY

ABOUT OPPORTUNITY PUBLISHING

I'm poet Guy Farmer and I created Opportunity Publishing to offer talented poets a chance to share their wonderful voices in a thoughtful, quality poetry anthology, free of charge. For more information, visit www.opportunitypublishing.com.

Made in the USA
San Bernardino, CA
31 May 2018